CORVETTE PROTOTYPES & SHOW CARS Photo Album

Edited by Wallace A. Wyss
Introduction by Dick Guldstrand

Iconografix
Photo Album Series

Iconografix continuously seeks collections of archival photographs for reproduction in future books. We require a minimum of 120 photographs per subject. We prefer subjects narrow in focus, i.e., a specific model, railroad, racing venue, etc. Photographs must be of high-quality, suited to reproduction in an 8x10-inch format. We willingly pay for the use of photographs.

If you own or know of such a collection, please contact: The Publisher, Iconografix, PO Box 446, Hudson, Wisconsin 54016.

Iconografix
PO Box 446
Hudson, Wisconsin 54016 USA

Text Copyright © 1997

Iconografix books are offered at a discount when sold in quantity for promotional use. Businesses or organizations seeking details should write to the Marketing Department, Iconografix, at the above address.

Library of Congress Card Number 97-70641

ISBN 1-882256-77-8

97 98 99 00 01 02 03 5 4 3 2 1

Printed in the United States of America

PREFACE

As with any car, every Corvette began as a concept—an idea. Actually, a great many ideas, as thousands of "engineered" bits and pieces go into every Corvette. Regardless of the ideas or their source, every one is tested before a car reaches production. *Corvette Prototypes and Show Cars Photo Album* features many of the prototypes and concept cars through which Corvette's designers (and Chevrolet and General Motors management) evaluated the styling and mechanical features—the ideas—that were considered for adoption on production Corvettes. A number of competition cars and modified production cars are also included, as often they also served as test rigs.

By pure happenstance of geography and a precocious interest in cars, it so happens that I have a personal connection to several of the cars in this book. Many years ago, I used to ride my bicycle over to the wealthy Detroit, Michigan suburb of Birmingham to shoot the breeze with this nice old man who had a lot of unusual cars. He didn't seem to care that I was but a teenager. The important thing was that I was a car guy and he was a car guy. He said that he liked guys "who had gasoline running in their veins." He liked to show off his cars. They weren't just ordinary cars. No, the cars lined up in Bill Mitchell's garage on Hamilton Drive were cars like the Mako Shark II, Corvair Monza GT, and the original Stingray. From time to time, I even visited Mr. Mitchell at the General Motors Tech Center. Sometimes, he would drop everything and send a message to the garage to get one of the cars ready. We would take a couple of laps on the test track behind the Design Center, the exhausts roaring and Mitchell pointing out this or that feature of the car.

I even talked to Zora Duntov a couple of times, and still later I met Larry Shinoda, the designer of the Stingray race car, the Shark, Mako Shark, and several other significant prototypes. Both men added further fuel to my interest in Corvette.

For almost 45 years, Corvette has reigned as the ultimate American sports car. It is a pleasure to provide a "peek behind the throne," at many of the ideas—good and bad; accepted and rejected—that have helped perpetuate its rule. This book is dedicated to the millions of loyal Corvette subjects. Long live the king!

I could not have proposed this book if it were not for the early encouragement in the subject provided by the late William L. Mitchell and the late Walter Mackenzie. I also thank Larry Shinoda and the following individuals and organizations for their contributions: photo researcher and ultimate Corvette enthusiast Duke Williams, for his research and interview of Charles M. Jordan; Mr. Jordan, for making his time and photo collection available; Chevrolet Public Relations, Thousand Oaks, California, for photos; *Automobile Quarterly*, for the loan of photos from their collection; John Gunnell of *Old Cars Weekly*, for artwork and photos from their collection; Kurtis Oblinger, whose photos taken at the Monterey Historics and Pebble Beach are among the classic racing images of the 20th Century; Rich Mason, for the loan of photos; Alan Kaplan, for the offer of items from his collection; Dayton Wire Wheel Products, for photos of the Curtice low-fin SR-2 and first generation XP-700; and special thanks to Mark Patrick and the National Automotive History Collection of the Detroit Public Library, an archive which serves car enthusiasts worldwide by continually building and sharing its storehouse of images and knowledge.

Wallace A. Wyss, Editor
Riverside, California
April 1997

FOREWORD

I was 11 years old when I first saw that red '58 'Vette, with its rollbar, blackwalls, and the sound of its fuel-injected 283 through the optional straight-through mufflers. What a sight! What a sound! I told my parents, "When I'm 16, I want a new Corvette." They replied, "Sure, if you earn the money, we'll let you buy one."

I soon added 14 lawn mowing jobs to my paper route, and put every dime I earned in the bank. As time passed, I was tantalized by Corvette show cars, which pointed the way to the Corvette I would someday own. The XP-700, although bizarre by today's standards, was a product of the Fifties, and I loved it. Then, the Stingray racer showed up, followed by the Shark, which really did preview the next Corvette.

As my 16th birthday approached, I had saved nearly $6,000, and I planned to buy a '62 327 "two-top" 'Vette. As the year wore on, rumors of a *new* Corvette circulated. I decided to wait. When the Sting Ray showed up in the magazines, and shortly thereafter in the showroom, I went into an absolute frenzy. It was sensational. Absolutely stunning! The lines of the Stingray racer and the Shark were there. The magnificent "boat tail" rear with the split back light. Forget the roadster. It would be the new "Aerocoupe" for me!

Finally, in February 1963, my Dad and I made it to a local Chevy dealer and ordered a new Sting Ray—a red-on-red Split Window Coupe (model 837), 340 hp special high performance engine (L76), close-ratio four-speed (M20), positraction axle with 3.08:1 ratio (G81), metallic brakes (J65), Wonderbar AM radio (U65), and whitewall tires (P92). I drove it to high school the first time on April Fool's Day. I hid it up by the fire station, but was obviously spotted during the morning drive. Rumors were rampant. "Did you buy a new Corvette?" was a constant question all day long. I just smiled and shrugged my shoulders as I do today, 34 years later, when people ask, "Did you really buy it new?" Yes, the car is still mine.

When Wallace Wyss asked me to help him research old Corvette show cars, I began looking through hundreds of photographs to select those which I felt represented the dream. Not just my dream, but the dream of the millions of Corvette enthusiasts around the world. What a thrill it was to look again at the cars that inspired me to own the real thing. For a few brief and fleeting moments, I was sixteen again with a brand new Sting Ray.

Duke Williams. Photo Researcher
Redondo Beach, California
March 1997

The downward facing spear of the side chrome, the air scoops on the cowl, and the door keyhole of the 1953 Corvette prototype were among the styling details that distinguished the show car, built for GM's Motorama, from the first production Corvette.

INTRODUCTION

GM Design and Chevrolet have strived to make the Corvette their technology showpiece throughout its 40-plus years of manufacture. In my opinion, Corvette has been the one car that has consistently embodied the best in GM engineering. Although a number of Corvette features originated elsewhere, the "technology transfer" has not always been one way. The men and women who designed or influenced the design of the Corvette may have "borrowed" from the competition, but often, too, they have anticipated and, consequently, set new trends.

Although we pay homage to the "designers," the Corvette has always been strongly influenced by the personality and will of the Design Director. When Harley Earl was in charge, the Corvette was one kind of car. When William L. Mitchell succeeded Earl, it became another kind of car. When Irv Rybacki followed Mitchell, there was a relatively quiet period. When he was succeeded by Chuck Jordan, a real enthusiast, an exciting period of new prototypes and show cars followed.

There have been, of course, engineers as well as designers involved in the Corvette story, and a battle for dominance was sometimes fought between the two groups. The most famous of the engineering "warriors" was Zora Arkus-Duntov, a Russian-born engineer with a love of racing. Zora was GM's resident enthusiast. The history of Corvette, from 1955 when he first joined the battle until he retired, was greatly influenced by Duntov's race car projects, some of which bordered on clandestine. Every once and a while (with or without GM management's support) he got his way, and an exciting new car was born—the Corvette SS, CERV I, CERV II, and the Grand Sport among them.

(Design and Engineering are not always at loggerheads. They sometimes put differences aside to join forces against GM's sometimes conservative management. The battle for the mid-engine Corvette, a significant part of this visual history, was just such a cause. Although heartily supported by Design and Engineering, those watching GM's financial interests considered the costs of tooling-up for the mid-engine cars too great; those concerned by the unwarranted fiasco over the rear-engined Corvair considered the potential of legal and public relations risks too great. We all know which factions prevailed in the end.)

Corvette Prototypes and Show Cars Photo Album includes many of my favorite Corvettes. It also features cars that some might consider less than "pure" Chevrolet Corvettes. Yet, outsiders have often been encouraged by GM, and their designs sometimes shared the show stand with the production cars and in-house concept cars. The Reynolds Corvette, which promoted the use of aluminum as a body material, was built on a chassis supplied by GM. Although ASC did not succeed in selling Chevrolet on the concept of their LT-1 Spyder, they did earn a contract to build the production car's removable hardtop. Pininfarina was supplied chassis at no cost, and the Rondine is just one example of their work sanctioned by GM. Even "parallel manufacturers" (for want of a better phrase), such as myself and my partner Detlef Stevenson, are encouraged and accepted by the factory. Being a long-time "Corvette guy" and an experienced racer, I drove a disguised C5 chassis for three years before the new Corvette's recent introduction, so that my opinion could be sampled.

What about future Corvettes? Although the likes of Earl, Mitchell, and Duntov are gone, there remain a number of brilliant and dedicated GM designers and engineers at work on tomorrow's Corvette. I've been around Corvettes a long time, and, as much as any Corvette enthusiast, I can hardly wait to see what's coming.

Dick Guldstrand
Guldstrand Enterprises
Culver City, California
March 1997

The 1953 prototype carried chrome script above the license plate frame that identified the car. "Corvette" script also appeared above the front grille. Both front and rear script were absent from the production car.

Three 1954 Motorama Corvette show cars (front to back): Corvair, Nomad, and a Corvette with removable hardtop and wind-up windows; and a 1954 production model.

The Corvette-based Nomad was a bold concept for an American automaker—a high-performance wagon. The roofline was used by Chevrolet on what became the Nomad, built from 1955 through 1957 but not on the Corvette chassis. The side exhaust ports on the lower rear rocker panels were toyed with on Corvette clay models, but were ultimately rejected.

The Corvair's fastback styling with chopped-off tail was influenced by European designs, the creators of which were more concerned with aerodynamics than were their American counterparts. Note the hood vents and front fender "gills," neither of which were carried over to the production Corvette.

The Corvette Sebring race cars of 1956 and 1957 influenced the styling and mechanical features of several subsequent competition cars, show cars, and production Corvettes. This photo was taken at Sebring in 1956.

Legend has it that Jerry Earl, son of GM Styling chief Harley Earl, yearned to race a Ferrari. Chevy already had the 1956 Sebring racers, but, to keep Jerry from "going foreign," Earl had his designers whip up a hotter looking Corvette for his son to race. Hence the SR-2, with its longer nose; fairing cones for the headlamps; fog lamps in place of turn signals; air scoop at the end of the body side cove; and tail-fin.

The SR-2 at Elkhart Lake, Wisconsin for the 1956 June Sprints. Originally, the top of the tail-fin was even with the top of the rear deck. After William L. Mitchell, Styling VP and Earl's eventual successor, had an SR-2 built with a taller fin integrated into a Jaguar D-type style of headrest (see page 14), the young Earl's car was returned to the styling center and redone in a similar fashion.

13

At least two "high-fin" SR-2s were built with this Jaguar D-type influenced-headrest fairing with integral tail fin. The wheels were Halibrand magnesium knock-offs, a favorite of dry lakes racers. The SR-2s were used to test various components, including the heavy-duty suspension system that became RPO684—heavy-duty springs, front anti-roll bar, Spicer-built positraction rear end, and faster steering.

The SR-2 was both a race car and a showpiece. The dashboard typified the glitzy approach to GM show cars of the time. Interior door panels were made from concave stainless steel, and featured a two-foot long rope-type door pull. The SR-2's show career came to an abrupt halt, after GM signed a pact with other Detroit automakers that forbade tie-ins with racing.

Rich Mason's SR-2, the ex-Earl car, reveals how designers dispensed with the production car bumpers. The trunk lid is hinged at the bottom, and swings down to reveal spare tire and rear-mounted battery. At least one SR-2 was fitted with a bubble-top for record runs on the packed sands of Daytona Beach (the track not having been built yet), where Buck Baker was clocked at 152.86 m.p.h. in the flying mile—almost as fast as a D-type Jag.

If ever there was a photograph that could have sold thousands of Corvettes had it been used in an ad, it would have been this photo of Dr. Dick Thompson about to start a race in an SR-2. Providing moral support was racer Betty Skelton, who earlier set a speed record of 137 m.p.h. in a Corvette Sebring racer at Daytona.

Harlow Curtice was president of GM during the period that the SR-2 was developed. This look-alike was built by GM's styling staff and presented to him. Curtice's car was fitted with Dayton wire wheels instead of the Halibrands used on the racers.

It took a bit of cut-and-fit to fit the hardtop over the tailfin of the Curtice car.

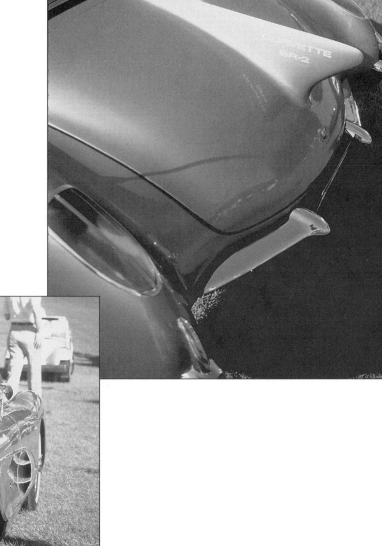

With the exception of the bumperettes and a bit of extra chrome trim, the front-end and hood treatments of the Curtice car matched those of the SR-2.

The Super Sport was a 1957 Corvette show car. Its twin racing windscreens and blue paint stripe over white evoked the image of the Sebring race cars. The front end treatment was stock Corvette; the scoop in the body side cove was pure SR-2.

Zora Arkus-Duntov, the Russian-born and German-educated engineer who championed the cause of Corvette racing for decades, at the wheel of the Corvette SS at Sebring in 1957. Duntov convinced Harley Earl that a race car based on the stock Corvette did not have a prayer of beating the Ferraris and Maseratis at Sebring, and that GM would have to develop a purpose-built racer. The SS was developed in only six months. In 1958, after its racing career ended, it was clocked at over 183 m.p.h.

The long tapered tail of the SS was a design advocated by the famous aerodynamicist Dr. Wunibald Kamm. The bubble-top was developed to meet some obscure racing rule, but at Sebring the car ran as an open roadster.

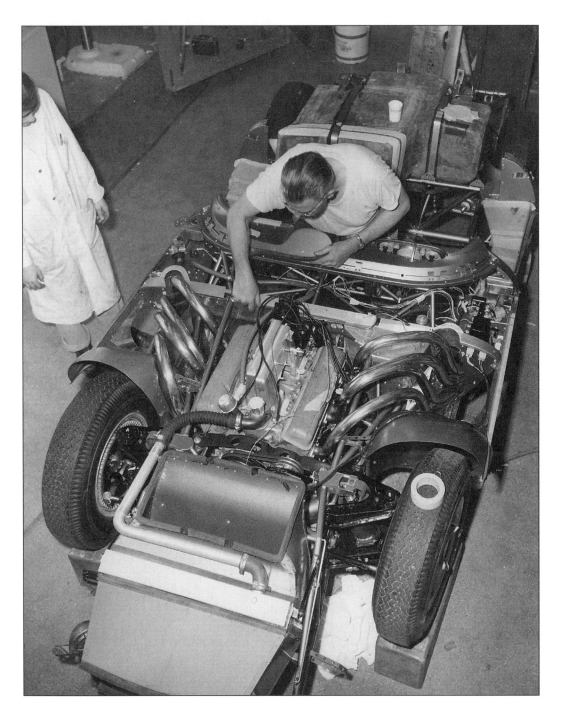

The 180-lb., chrome-moly, tubular-bar space frame of the SS was built along the lines of that of the Mercedes 300SL. Rear axle was DeDion; drum brakes were from Chrysler.

The busy interior of the SS shows the cobbled nature of a race car. Seats had some side support.

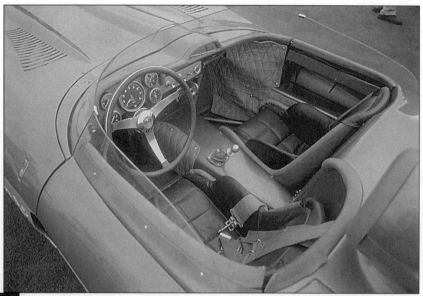

The SS engine was a 283 iron-block, with aluminum cylinder heads and Ramjet fuel injection, rated at 307 hp at 6,400 rpm. The headers were tailored to individual lengths, and the bodywork designed to accommodate them. As with the earlier Sebring racers and the SR-2, the SS rode on Halibrand knock-off mags.

Duntov, right, explains the features of the SS to racer John Fitch. Fitch and Pierro Taruffi were drafted to drive at Sebring, after Stirling Moss and Juan Fangio, both of whom had driven an earlier mule, chose other rides.

Bill Mitchell had "customs" built for himself, even before his predecessor retired. The first was his version of the SR-2. Another such dream car was this "Mitchell-ized" street Corvette, the XP-700. The "lakes pipes" were fitted in the space left by removal of the rocker panel area. The tail previewed that of the upcoming 1961-62 Corvette. The elliptical grille cavity strongly resembled that of a one-off Ferrari 250 GT (see inset photo), wrought by Pininfarina.

The Mitchell custom received the blessing of management, and traveled the show car circuit in this form. The grille cavity was refashioned in a more elliptical shape, and the car was re-sprayed metallic gold. The front under-tray air scoop seems inspired by aircraft design.

Harley Earl liked bubble-tops, hence the XP-700's "double-bubble" Plexiglas top. Headlights were Lucas "flame thrower" road lamps. This was one of many Corvette show cars fitted with Dayton wire wheels.

The rear of XP-700 incorporated vertical bumperettes, an idea that never took hold on production Corvettes. Horizontal slits in the band separating roof bubbles were for cockpit ventilation. Atop the band was the "periscope" rear-view mirror, a Mitchell favorite used on several prototypes.

The vertical side vents of the XP-700 were probably inspired by those on Ferraris. The "cutaway" front fender—for better brake cooling—was also an idea from Italy, first seen on Jim Kimberley's one-off Pininfarina-designed Ferrari 375 MM. Functional side exhausts later became optional on production Corvettes.

The interior of the XP-700 retained much from the 1958 production Corvette, except for different steering wheel, the metal grid in the foot well area, and the chronometric stopwatch set into the console, an idea Mitchell probably picked up from Pininfarina, who installed the same instrument in some Ferrari Superamericas. The second smaller shift lever controlled an experimental overdrive.

In 1959, the bones of the SS were revived when Mitchell secretly funded the Stingray race car. Mitchell purchased the chassis of the 1957 SS race car mule for $500, and had Larry Shinoda, his "personal" designer, create a new body. The shape was inspired by the 1957 Ghia IXG Turin show car, an enclosed-body dragster designed by American Tom Tjaarda. The key feature was the sharp-peaked wheelwell housings rising above the body's upper surface. Livery was silver, although Mitchell had it re-sprayed red at least twice—once for an opening scene of an Elvis Presley movie. The inset photo reveals the car's interior.

The potent nose of the Stingray race car incorporated functional hood air vents. Note fog lamps behind the grille. This shot was taken by the famed photographer Kurtis Oblinger at the Monterey Historics in 1989, long after the car was retired from racing.

The rear view of the Stingray shows the upswept tail. The car suffered so much wear-and-tear during its short racing career that it was re-bodied at least once. (One historian writes that one body was built from silk cloth reinforced with balsa wood). Chief cause of damage to the car was inadequate brakes, which, at times, forced driver Dr. Dick Thompson to slow down by bashing into the cars in front of him! Thompson won the SCCA C-modified championship three times with the car.

The Stingray was raced on Mitchell's own nickel. Here it starts off against two Scarabs, aluminum-bodied, Corvette-powered race cars built by Lance Reventlow. (Mitchell was such a fan of Reventlow that he later hired Reventlow's key man to run his own dream car shop.)

Two years after the SS, Duntov came back with CERV I (Chevrolet Engineering Research Vehicle I), ostensibly a test rig used to evaluate such things as rear suspension configurations and anti-lock brakes. The tubular-framed single-seater was built along Indy car lines. It weighed 1,450 lbs., and was powered by a 350-hp 283. The alloy-block motor was joined by other lightweight parts, including a magnesium bellhousing and clutch housing. Duntov frequently changed its engine, at one point reaching a configuration that clocked over 200 m.p.h.

Larry Shinoda, right, with a full-size rendering of his design for a Corvette built on the Corvair chassis. At left is Ron Hill, who later became Chairman of Transportation Design at the Art Center College of Design. The photo is dated November 9, 1959.

Two clay models were made of Shinoda's design. This one, with long rear deck lid blister, was intended for a V-8-powered car; the other for a flat-six. The long rear deck and unusual headrest fairings were later used on the Corvair Super Spyder show car, also designed by Shinoda.

The teardrop shape of the 1963 Sting Ray Coupe is considered a classic. What were its origins? Some suspect that it was strongly influenced by this one-off 1955 Alfa Romeo 3500 Disco Volante built by Boano, the Italian coachbuilder, for Argentine dictator Juan Peron.

Look closely at the two Sting Ray prototypes appearing behind the Stingray race car. Note the simulated side vents on the doors. This photo was taken in 1960, two years before production of the Sting Ray was announced. The side vents made it to the production car, but were reversed and moved forward to the front fender.

The 1961 XP-755 Shark was a Mitchell concept, designed by Shinoda, with Earl's influence apparent in the double-bubble top carried over from the XP 700. The rear deck lid carried little flip-up doors that were part of an elaborate emergency brake lamp system (see inset photo). The chrome scoop atop the bubble housed the rear-view periscope.

A Tale of Two Noses. The original Shark incorporated vents for the supercharger hump and lettering proclaiming "SUPERCHARGER". The grille was very vulnerable.

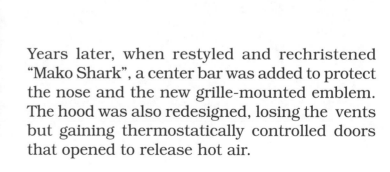

Years later, when restyled and rechristened "Mako Shark", a center bar was added to protect the nose and the new grille-mounted emblem. The hood was also redesigned, losing the vents but gaining thermostatically controlled doors that opened to release hot air.

The interior of the early Shark picked-up on XP-700 themes, such as the chrome gridwork foot wells and chronometer mounted on the floor console. Similarities between the two cars were no accident. According to Mark Jordan, son of GM designer Charles M. Jordan, the Shark was built on the XP-700, thus explaining its disappearance forevermore. The wood-rimmed steering wheel was given to Mitchell by Enzo Ferrari— explanation enough for its use.

The interior of the Mako Shark was far more modern in appearance than that of the Shark. The new layout clustered six gauges in a center binnacle. Here, the dash is simulated wood, but the editor recalls having seen the car on one occasion with a black "crackle" finish to this same dash.

The Mako Shark was fitted with wheels similar in style to those of the Chaparral, but, as the absence of bolts around the circumference indicate, the rims were not demountable from the center section.

Duntov attempted to return GM to racing in 1963 with the Grand Sport. A lightweight Sting Ray road car look-alike, it was built on a special frame and with an ultra-thin body. Duntov planned to build the necessary 100 units to homologate it as a production car with the FIA, but GM killed production plans after only five cars were built. The five survivors made it into the hands of racers, who campaigned them on their own. Here, a Grand Sport struts its stuff in December 1963 at Nassau, where GS coupes finished first and third in class—blowing Carroll Shelby's highly touted Cobras out of the water.

The Grand Sport only superficially resembled production Corvettes. The back window shape was different, and a functional trunk lid was fitted. The scoop on the rear deck was for the differential cooler.

The original plan called for a 377-cubic-inch, twin-plug, alloy-block V-8 but when forced to dispose of the cars quickly, Duntov shipped them to racers *sans* engines. They installed iron block engines. The owner of this GS has nearly managed to replicate the original carburetor set-up of four side-draft Webers.

Grand Sport dashboards were, again, only roughly similar to those of production Corvettes.

This lightly modified Sting Ray roadster, probably a '64, has Shark-style side pipes with exposed mufflers. It appeared in at least one major car show. Mark Jordan recalls it as one of several cars—all with white hood stripe treatment—built for GM executive "Bunkie" Knudsen. It was photographed at the Meadowbrook Concours in Rochester Hills, Michigan. Even in Detroit, it is an example of a rare breed—a GM factory show car that is now in private hands.

Another 1964 modified production show car, built for Mrs. William L. Mitchell and now part of a California museum collection. The editor remembers seeing this car tooling around on Detroit's Woodward Avenue in the mid-60s. Exposed side pipe treatment mimics Giorgetto Giugiaro's 1963 Iso Grifo A3/L prototype done for Bertone (see inset photo).

The Corvette Rondine show car was built by Pininfarina on a production 1963 Sting Ray chassis. Two rooflines were tried: an inward slanting rear window with the roof cut off at the B-pillar; and the sloping rear window shown here.

Any resemblance between the rear fenders of the Rondine and those of the Fiat 124 are a matter of lineage. Both cars were designed by Tom Tjaarda, the Michigan native who had worked for Italian *carrozzerie* since 1959.

The 4WD CERV II was another attempt by Duntov to build a limited series of race cars. Designers were Shinoda and Tony Lapine, the latter would one day head up design for Porsche. The project was nipped in the bud after only two cars were built. The car shown was fitted with two torque converters, fore and aft, similar to the type tested in the Chaparral. The crude bodywork betrays its origins as an Engineering-based project. The inset photo of a CERV II clay model reveals a more stylish design than that which was adopted. This car, donated to the Cunningham Museum by GM, is now in private hands.

The mid-engine Corvette GS-IIb, designed by Shinoda and built by Frank Winchell's R&D staff, strongly resembled Shinoda's designs for the Corvair SS and Monza GT prototypes. This car, with alloy chassis, was the second of two cars built. GS-II, the first car, was built on a steel chassis.

The original non-running "clay" of the Mako Shark II, introduced in 1965, had a wicked-looking side exhaust. It was one of the first uses of the flat-black vs. chrome treatment that swept the world's automakers in the 1970s. Lettering on the hood hump read "MARK IV 396" to signify use of a "big block" Corvette engine. Tires were Firestone Indys, thin-walled racing rubber not practical for the street, but, nevertheless, the hottest thing you could run on your street car in 1965.

The Mako Shark II's roof lifted for better access and was removable for pace car duties. This led to the removable roof hatches in the 1968-1982 Corvettes.

The "running" Mako Shark II had a potent look. Paintwork was similar to that of the earlier Shark: dark on the top and white at the bottom, with a gentle fogging of the two colors in between. The 1968 production Corvette carried a similar profile, except that the roofline did not taper to a point at the rear. The lines of the production car were less crisp, and, of course, the purity of the design was sullied by bumpers.

Warren Olson, former-Scarab team member then working for Mitchell, shows *Hot Rod*'s Eric Dahlquist the details of the Mako Shark II engine. Note the closed "gills" in front of the wheel arch. The flaps opened when turning corners to reveal cornering lamps.

The engine of the Mako Shark II varied at Mitchell's whim. Here, it was the Mark IV 427. Later, it was an alloy-block ZL-1.

The Mako Shark II did not offer much front bumper protection. Headlamp covers slid back into the body to reveal fixed-in-place French-made lenses.

Although the roofline's side profile was picked up by the production Sting Ray of 1968-1982, its rear taper was not. The rear louvers went flat at the touch of a button.

The rectangular exhausts on the running car were a work of art—doubtless, too expensive for production.

Gadgetry abounded on the Mako Shark II. The rear bumper extended at the touch of a button. The rear spoiler, likewise. Even the license plate revolved. Shades of James Bond!

The interior of the Mako Shark II clay model featured an airplane-style steering wheel, plethora of gauges, form-fitting bucket seats, and floor grid from XP-700 in more discreet form. Note roller thumbwheels on console.

The interior on the running car showed reversion to boring old steering wheel, and very flat looking upholstery. The gauges were replaced by one of GM's first experiments with digital readout dashboards. Note redesign of console.

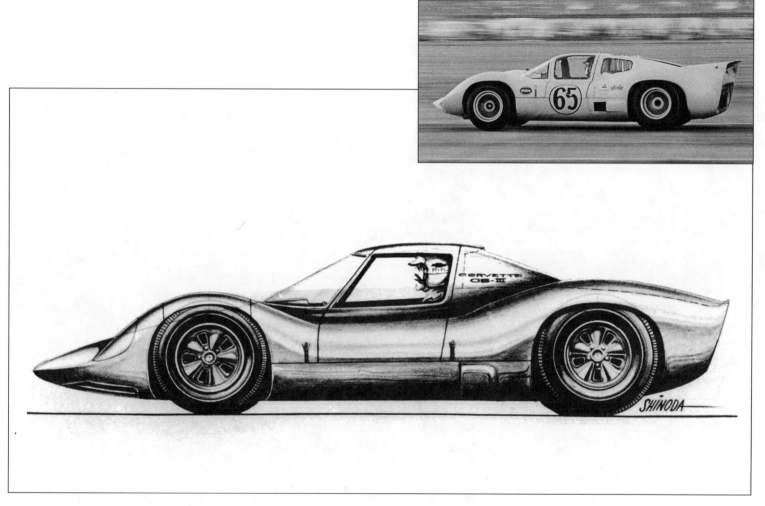

Note the resemblance between the Shinoda-designed, mid-engine Corvette GS-III and one version of Jim Hall's Chaparral.

Frank Winchell's R&D group considered various engine configurations for Corvette. One result that translated to a prototype was the XP-819, a rear-engine car developed in the early to mid-sixties. Styling was by Shinoda.

The functional hood vent of the XP-819 allowed air that passed through the front-mounted radiator to exit. The XP-819's styling was also used on another Shinoda design, the Corvair Monza SS (see inset photo).

The Astro-Vette of 1968 was pure car show schmaltz. It resurrected a couple of 1930's concepts in aerodynamics: flat, low-drag wheel covers, and rear fender skirts (hinged at the top for access to wheel). Cutlines on the front fender were probably meant to simulate flaps that could open to release hot air from underneath the hood.

The XP-880, an updated XP-819, was another Winchell project. This time the engine was mounted amidships. It handled better than the XP-819 but still required wider wheels and tires at the rear. The entire rear section lifted to allow access to the engine. The lack of headlamps and awkward blending of features is characteristic of an internal project not intended for public viewing. This engineering mule was dolled-up for show, when it later toured the circuit as the "Astro II".

The 1969 Manta Ray was the Mako Shark II reborn. Note the addition of a front spoiler and halfhearted attempt at grille protection. Side pipes reappeared, although they were less dramatic than the Mako Shark II's originals. Hood hump now sports "ZL-1" script.

The transformation from Mako Shark II to Manta Ray saw the rear window louvers eliminated in favor of a flat rear deck. The "mail slot" rear window gave the car a very California-custom "chopped top" look. The bobbed tail of the Mako Shark II gave way to a long tapered energy-absorbing tail. As on the Shark, when the driver hit the brakes extra hard, little doors on the rear deck popped open and reflected light from a pair of upward-facing stop lamps.

The Sirocco, a Mitchell-modified production car for his own use. The car had cast alloy "lace" wheels, his usual roof periscope, body-colored trim, and front and rear spoilers. The chrome emblem on the fender indicates the car was fitted with the potent ZL-1 427-cubic-inch aluminum engine, developed for Can-Am racers and offered as an option on 1969 production Corvettes.

The Aero Coupe of 1969 was another "Mitchell-ized" street car, this one testing new concepts in spoilers and an alternative design for the side-mount exhausts offered on production Corvettes. The one-piece roof hatch was hinged at the rear and swung up to ease entrance and exit, *à la* Mako Shark II.

The Mulsanne show car was the Aero Coupe re-worked and more heavily customized. Named for the straightaway on the famous Le Mans race circuit, it featured fixed-in-place headlamps behind transparent covers, two Stingray race car-styled deep indentations in the front hood feeding air to functional scoops, a ZL-1 engine, and high-mounted side mirrors.

Another lightly modified production show car, the Turbo Corvette, carried a turbocharged V-6. The car appeared in the era of growing concern over M.P.G. figures, and it was hoped that a turbo V-6 would offer the power of a V-8 yet deliver better gas mileage. A second Turbo Corvette show car was built, but without hood vents. Similar graphics were used on the 1982 Collector Edition production car.

The XP-882 followed the XP-880/Astro II, and was a more innovative mid-engine design. Its transversely mounted 400-cubic-inch V-8 was mated to a three-speed Turbo Hydramatic transmission, using an Oldsmobile Toronado transaxle. The bumper styling was a bit of a mismatch—a new-style Endura soft bumper at the rear, but old fashioned chrome at the front. The circular lids allowed access for refill of fluids.

The XP-882 was an attractive car for the period, and was reportedly slated for production at one time. It made the show car circuit, after Chevrolet's General Manager John DeLorean learned that Ford planned to unveil the Pantera prototype at the 1970 New York Auto Show. Car magazines soon speculated that the XP-882 was the upcoming 1973 Corvette. Alas, it was not.

The Return of the Mako Shark II Boat-tail. Venetian blinds on the rear deck allowed hot engine air to escape while keeping rain water out, just as on the Lamborghini Miura.

The crudeness of the interior of the XP-882 reflects its original status as an "engineering" test rig and not a show car. Pontiac enthusiasts will recognize the Trans-Am steering wheel.

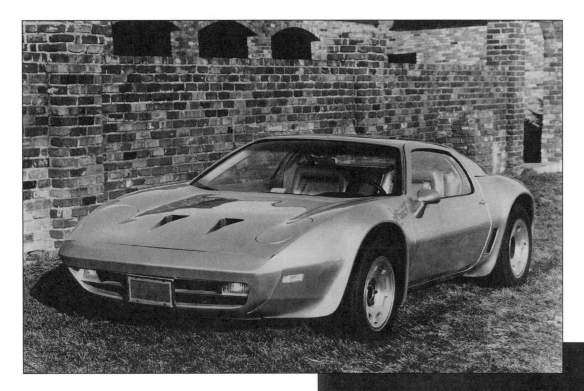

XP-895, the Reynolds Corvette, was fitted with a transversely mounted 400-cubic-inch V-8, mated to a Turbo Hydramatic via a bevel box. Suspension was coil all around. Headlights rolled over *à la* Opel GT.

The XP-895 was an unusual case, even by Corvette standards. It was built for Reynolds Aluminum on an extra XP-882 chassis. Designed by GM and built by an outside firm, its aluminum construction was meant to convince GM of the practicality of aluminum as a body material. They failed to win their case. Corvettes are still made from various plastics.

From the rear, there is a suggestion of the Manta Ray roofline on the XP-895. The car featured two rear deck lids, similar to those on the Ferrari Dino: one for the engine; one for the luggage compartment.

The design drawing of the XP-897 Corvette show car, known as the "Two Rotor". XP-897 carried GM's version of the Wankel (rotary) engine. Styling was fresh, except for quad headlights matching those of the Chevrolet Monza, the mass-volume, front-engined car designed for GM rotary power.

The clay model of the Two Rotor. The rear roofline profile may have influenced that of the production Camaro.

In metal, the Two Rotor carried smaller diameter wheel rims than designers had hope for. Body fabrication was executed by Pininfarina. The car made its show debut in Frankfurt in September 1973.

The best view of the XP-892 was from the rear. Its hatch covered both the engine and luggage compartments. Note the subtle air extraction vents above the rear window, and the XP-882-style rear three-quarter window. The editor drove this car, and enjoyed its rotary exhaust note and flawless workmanship.

The interior of the Two Rotor was first class, and illustrates the difference between an "engineering" car, cobbled together for in-house evaluation, and one designed from the beginning as a show car.

The engine of the Two Rotor was mounted transversely. The luggage area was immediately behind the engine compartment.

Design renderings of the proposed Four Rotor Corvette. The Four Rotor appeared at the same time as the Two Rotor. It was powered by two twin-rotors harnessed together by a chain drive.

The Four Rotor's Gullwing-type doors were not unique, however, the bi-fold design was. Note the hidden A-pillar covered by wraparound glass. Charles M. Jordan supervised the design.

The Four Rotor advancing from paper to clay. Clay is kept warm so it remains easy to sculpt. After the shape is finalized it can be coated with a thin film to simulate paint. On the wall are numerous drawings that show earlier conceptions of the car.

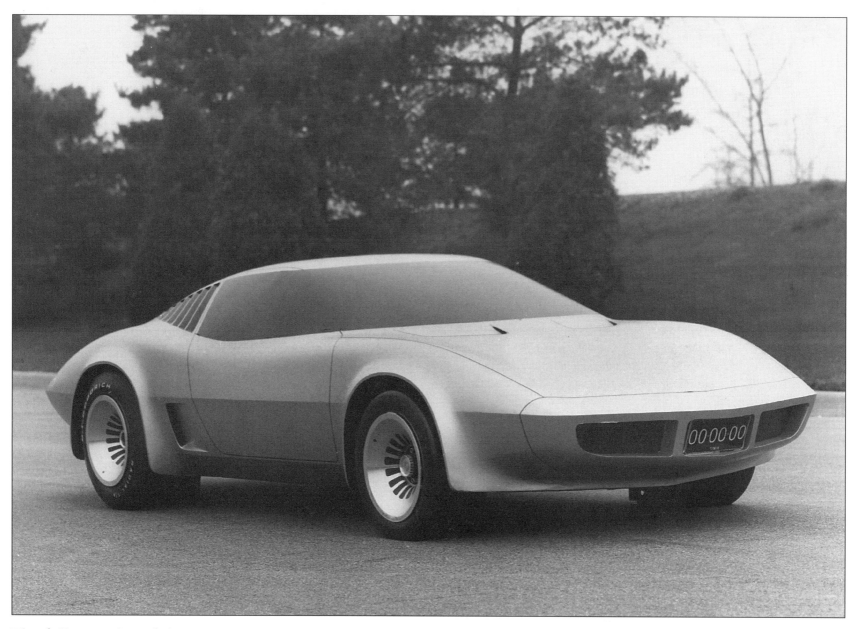

The full-size clay of the Four Rotor. The running car was built on an XP-882 chassis. The grille shared a strong resemblance to that of the production Corvette, however, in the final form it did not. Wheels were similar in style to Alfa 33 racing wheels.

The Four Rotor in finished form. The design called for a soft nose and tail. The rear deck lid incorporated panels that, presumably, would open when the temperature of the engine compartment reached a certain level. After the GM rotary engine program was scrapped, a Chevy pushrod V-8 was installed in the car and it was renamed the "Aero-Vette".

The finished Four Rotor prototype with doors fully opened. The bi-fold design kept the open doors from extending beyond the width of the body. Because of the low door sill, ease of entry and exit was excellent.

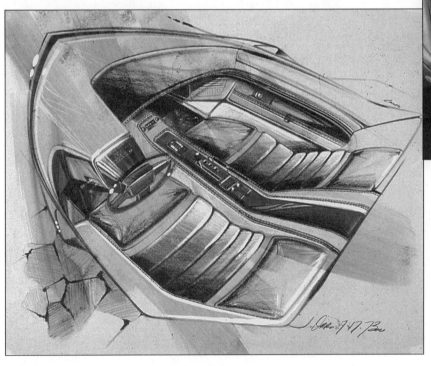

The interior of the Four Rotor featured the "pre-wrinkled leather" look popular in Italy at the time. Although modern, it was less flamboyant than the interior shown in the original concept drawing.

A dream assignment went to Corvette designer Randy Wittine, when he was asked to come up with a body shape for a Lola T-600 coupe. Corvette or not, it was *called* the GTP Corvette, wore the Chevy bow tie, and, at least on paper, carried a Corvette-type nose and Corvette-style wheels.

The actual Corvette GTP bore even less resemblance to the Corvette. Two cars were built, one with a V-8 the other with a turbo V-6, and were raced by private teams. The undertray incorporated "ground effects" tunnels to generate downforce—much more than could ever be designed into a practical road car.

"Bespoke tailoring" is what your Saville Row tailor calls hand-cutting pieces of cloth for a suit made to match the measured form of an individual customer. Construction methods are much the same with prototype cars. Here, Bertone craftsmen form and piece together the Ramarro show car.

Bertone of Italy built at least two Corvette show cars. The 1984 Ramarro was built on the new Corvette chassis. Here, model makers translate the Ramarro scale model into a full-size model.

The lime green Ramarro's chief contribution to passenger car design was the use of sliding doors, which in America are something considered only for van use. The car sported a more "air-penetrating" nose than that of the stock Corvette, by virtue of its radiator and A/C condenser having been relocated to the rear. One wonders if that would have effected cooling. The Ramarro also had an unusual seat, almost like a saddle draped across the central console tunnel.

In the mid-'80s, GM's Design Vice President, Charles M. Jordan, commissioned Cecomp of Italy to build this full-scale clay model of the Corvette Indy, a mid-engine show car that would carry a prototype 265-cubic-inch Indy car racing engine.

Among features planned for the Indy were all-wheel drive, four-wheel steering, traction control, twin turbos, air-to-air intercoolers, and active suspension. Of course, with a non-running clay model you can *plan* anything.

The Indy clay model in open targa form.

The interior view of the Indy clay revealed an engine. Nonetheless, it was not a running car. Note the dramatic rake to the windscreen.

The dashboard featured a digital gauge for speedometer, bar graph for tach, and rear-view TV screen. The monitor at right was part of the ETAK navigation system, later made optional in Buicks.

The running Corvette Indy, unveiled in 1988, was powered by the code-named "350/32" engine, a 32-valve, 4-cam V-8 rated at 380 hp at 6,000 rpm (early version of the production ZR-1/LT-5 engine), rather than the Indy racing engine. Designers pulled back a little on the exaggerated lines of the non-runner with less overhang in front and exposed headlamps. The T-bar roof offered greater rigidity. Flow-through rear deck spoiler of the clay was retained.

The "futuristic" interior of the running Corvette Indy changed little from that of the clay model.

CERV III was built concurrently with the Indy, and was produced by GM Corporate Engineering. Lotus acted as consultant on engineering and construction. The object was to take the Indy "dream car" design and produce a "roadable" car. One practical step was to drop the severely curved side windows that prevented roll-up windows. Also, the nose was shortened. Rated at 650 h.p., the ZR-1/LT-5 engine was fitted with twin Garret turbos. CERV III was tested on GM tracks in Michigan and Arizona, as well as on the Lotus track in Hethel, England. Only the roofline of CERV III reached the next generation Corvette.

The Indy and CERV III designs aside, Corvette show cars were few in the 1980s. Several outside firms offered suggestions, some hoping that their ideas would be adopted and that they would earn supplier contracts. ASC of Southgate, Michigan was among the most prolific. Their 1988 Geneve strongly suggested a direction GM could take with the next generation Corvette. The front was smoothed out with a built-in spoiler. The rear offered flush taillamps and integral spoiler; the side, different vents and a smoother look.

In 1990, Bertone created the Nivola, a mid-engine roadster with removable hardtop. Bertone built the model in foam (above), rather than clay, and then constructed a running car in metal (right), building on a metal surface plate to make sure everything lined up perfectly.

Nivola's suspension was hydropneumatic, adjusting to the load and to the road surface. Bertone mated the ZR-1/LT-5 engine to a ZF five-speed, the same employed in the Pantera. The hardtop lid was stored above the crowded engine compartment. Foot-wide doors incorporated luggage bins. The car owed a lot in styling to the earlier Lamborghini Athon show car. Bertone, designers of the Miura and Countach, had built 18 mid-engine show cars prior to the Nivola.

ASC, the company that made millions installing sunroofs in the cars of the Big Three and later building convertibles for Chevrolet, Pontiac, and Porsche, earnestly tried to help Chevrolet "over the hump" of not being able to decide on styling to follow the shape introduced in 1984. In this 1990 proposal, they show the ZR-1 Corvette with a cutdown frameless windscreen, headrest "bumps" on the convertible top boot, and a modified hood with functional vents.

With Chevrolet's help, ASC went the next step and built a running ZR-1-based spyder, with taller windscreen than shown in the drawing, different side vents, and a Porsche Speedster-style roof. GM, however, refused to offer the LT-5 engine for use in an open Corvette. Ironically, Advanced Engineering chief Don Runkle had more than a half-dozen examples built for testing, although without the chopped-top look. ASC's efforts were not all in vain. When it came time to offer a hardtop for the Corvette convertible, ASC won the contract.

ASC's ZR-1 also had a hardtop that ingeniously followed the lines of their racing-style side windows but offered a more conventional back window.

The ASC ZR-1's interior featured body-colored center console and small "hoops" that suggested roll bars, which, dare we suggest, may have inspired those on Ferrari's F50.

ASC's LT-1 spyder presented a more affordable solution for updating the Corvette. It would have required fewer changes to the body; a new convertible top boot; a different center console; the addition of a divider in the cockpit.

Stingray III was developed at the now-defunct Advanced Concept Center in Thousand Oaks, California. From the side, the car had a Porsche character to the soft top. The short hood length was possible only because of the car's V-6. (Perhaps that explains why it lacks "Corvette" proportions.) Although the car did not reach production as a Corvette, its basic shape was used by Chevrolet for the Cavalier convertible.

The strong wheels were a perfect contrast to the smooth body of the Stingray III. The thin headlight slits would be adopted in modified form for more than one GM car. The design world at large seems to have embraced body curve-following exposed lamps. Ironically, when the new generation Corvette arrived in 1997, it sported more mundane closed headlamps.

The Stingray III's four taillamps offered some continuity with past Corvettes. The rear undertray spoiler was for "ground effects."

The editor wishes to credit the National Automotive History Collection of the Detroit Public Library for the photos it contributed. Photos on pages 6, 19, 22, 40, 41 (upper right), 92, 93, 95 (both), and 105 (both) are part of the NAHC collection, and are used with their permission.

————————————

The editor seeks archival photos of Corvette prototypes, show cars, and factory race cars for possible inclusion in a future edition of this book or for use in a new work. Parties willing to loan, sell, or trade such photos may contact: Wallace A. Wyss, Box 55095, Riverside, California 92517 USA.

The Iconografix Photo Archive Series includes:

AMERICAN CULTURE

AMERICAN SERVICE STATIONS 1935-1943	ISBN 1-882256-27-1
COCA-COLA: A HISTORY IN PHOTOGRAPHS 1930-1969	ISBN 1-882256-46-8
COCA-COLA: ITS VEHICLES IN PHOTOGRAPHS 1930-1969	ISBN 1-882256-47-6
PHILLIPS 66 1945-1954	ISBN 1-882256-42-5

AUTOMOTIVE

FERRARI PININFARINA 1952-1996	ISBN 1-882256-65-4
GT40	ISBN 1-882256-64-6
IMPERIAL 1955-1963	ISBN 1-882256-22-0
IMPERIAL 1964-1968	ISBN 1-882256-23-9
LE MANS 1950: THE BRIGGS CUNNINGHAM CAMPAIGN	ISBN 1-882256-21-2
LINCOLN MOTOR CARS 1920-1942	ISBN 1-882256-57-3
LINCOLN MOTOR CARS 1946-1960	ISBN 1-882256-58-1
MG 1945-1964	ISBN 1-882256-52-2
MG 1965-1980	ISBN 1-882256-53-0
PACKARD MOTOR CARS 1935-1942	ISBN 1-882256-44-1
PACKARD MOTOR CARS 1946-1958	ISBN 1-882256-45-X
SEBRING 12-HOUR RACE 1970	ISBN 1-882256-20-4
STUDEBAKER 1933-1942	ISBN 1-882256-24-7
STUDEBAKER 1946-1958	ISBN 1-882256-25-5
VANDERBILT CUP RACE 1936 & 1937	ISBN 1-882256-66-2

TRACTORS AND CONSTRUCTION EQUIPMENT

CASE TRACTORS 1912-1959	ISBN 1-882256-32-8
CATERPILLAR MILITARY TRACTORS VOLUME 1	ISBN 1-882256-16-6
CATERPILLAR MILITARY TRACTORS VOLUME 2	ISBN 1-882256-17-4
CATERPILLAR SIXTY	ISBN 1-882256-05-0
CATERPILLAR THIRTY	ISBN 1-882256-04-2
CLETRAC AND OLIVER CRAWLERS	ISBN 1-882256-43-3
ERIE SHOVEL	ISBN 1-882256-69-7
FARMALL CUB	ISBN 1-882256-71-9
FARMALL F–SERIES	ISBN 1-882256-02-6
FARMALL MODEL H	ISBN 1-882256-03-4
FARMALL MODEL M	ISBN 1-882256-15-8
FARMALL REGULAR	ISBN 1-882256-14-X
FARMALL SUPER SERIES	ISBN 1-882256-49-2
FORDSON 1917-1928	ISBN 1-882256-33-6
HART-PARR	ISBN 1-882256-08-5
HOLT TRACTORS	ISBN 1-882256-10-7
INTERNATIONAL TRACTRACTOR	ISBN 1-882256-48-4
INTERNATIONAL TD CRAWLERS 1933-1962	ISBN 1-882256-72-7
JOHN DEERE MODEL A	ISBN 1-882256-12-3
JOHN DEERE MODEL B	ISBN 1-882256-01-8
JOHN DEERE MODEL D	ISBN 1-882256-00-X
JOHN DEERE 30 SERIES	ISBN 1-882256-13-1
MINNEAPOLIS-MOLINE U-SERIES	ISBN 1-882256-07-7
OLIVER TRACTORS	ISBN 1-882256-09-3
RUSSELL GRADERS	ISBN 1-882256-11-5
TWIN CITY TRACTOR	ISBN 1-882256-06-9

RAILWAYS

CHICAGO, ST. PAUL, MINNEAPOLIS & OMAHA RAILWAY 1880-1940	ISBN 1-882256-67-0
CHICAGO&NORTH WESTERN RAILWAY 1975-1995	ISBN 1-882256-76-X
GREAT NORTHERN RAILWAY 1945-1970	ISBN 1-882256-56-5
MILWAUKEE ROAD 1850-1960	ISBN 1-882256-61-1
SOO LINE 1975-1992	ISBN 1-882256-68-9
WISCONSIN CENTRAL LIMITED 1987-1996	ISBN 1-882256-75-1

TRUCKS

BEVERAGE TRUCKS 1910-1975	ISBN 1-882256-60-3
BROCKWAY TRUCKS 1948-1961*	ISBN 1-882256-55-7
DODGE TRUCKS 1929-1947	ISBN 1-882256-36-0
DODGE TRUCKS 1948-1960	ISBN 1-882256-37-9
LOGGING TRUCKS 1915-1970	ISBN 1-882256-59-X
MACK® MODEL AB*	ISBN 1-882256-18-2
MACK AP SUPER-DUTY TRUCKS 1926-1938*	ISBN 1-882256-54-9
MACK MODEL B 1953-1966 VOLUME 1*	ISBN 1-882256-19-0
MACK MODEL B 1953-1966 VOLUME 2*	ISBN 1-882256-34-4
MACK EB-EC-ED-EE-EF-EG-DE 1936-1951*	ISBN 1-882256-29-8
MACK EH-EJ-EM-EQ-ER-ES 1936-1950*	ISBN 1-882256-39-5
MACK FC-FCSW-NW 1936-1947*	ISBN 1-882256-28-X
MACK FG-FH-FJ-FK-FN-FP-FT-FW 1937-1950*	ISBN 1-882256-35-2
MACK LF-LH-LJ-LM-LT 1940-1956 *	ISBN 1-882256-38-7
MACK MODEL B FIRE TRUCKS 1954-1966*	ISBN 1-882256-62-X
MACK MODEL CF FIRE TRUCKS 1967-1981*	ISBN 1-882256-63-8
STUDEBAKER TRUCKS 1927-1940	ISBN 1-882256-40-9
STUDEBAKER TRUCKS 1941-1964	ISBN 1-882256-41-7

* This product is sold under license from Mack Trucks, Inc. All rights reserved.

The Iconografix Photo Album Series includes:

CORVETTE PROTOTYPES & SHOW CARS	ISBN 1-882256-77-8
LOLA RACE CARS 1962-1990	ISBN 1-882256-73-5
McLAREN RACE CARS 1965-1996	ISBN 1-882256-74-3

The Iconografix Photo Gallery Series includes:

CATERPILLAR PHOTO GALLERY	ISBN 1-882256-70-0

All Iconografix books are available from direct mail specialty book dealers and bookstores worldwide, or can be ordered from the publisher. For book trade and distribution information or to add your name to our mailing list contact

Iconografix
PO Box 446
Hudson, Wisconsin, 54016

Telephone: (715) 381-9755
(800) 289-3504 (USA)
Fax: (715) 381-9756

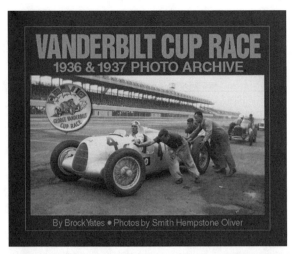

VANDERBILT CUP RACE
1936 & 1937 PHOTO ARCHIVE

By Brock Yates • Photos by Smith Hempstone Oliver

MORE
GREAT BOOKS FROM
ICONOGRAFIX

VANDERBILT CUP RACE 1936 & 1937
Photo Archive ISBN 1-882256-66-2

FERRARI PININFARINA 1952-1996
Photo Archive ISBN 1-88225665-4

GT40 *Photo Archive*
ISBN 1-882256-64-6

LOLA RACE CARS 1962-1990
Photo Album ISBN 1-882256-73-5

LEMANS 1950: THE BRIGGS CUNNINGHAM CAMPAIGN
Photo Archive ISBN 1-882256-21-2

McLAREN RACE CARS 1965-1996
Photo Album ISBN 1-882256-74-3

SEBRING 12-HOUR RACE 1970
Photo Arhive ISBN 1-882256-20-4

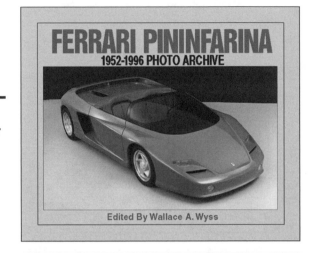

FERRARI PININFARINA
1952-1996 PHOTO ARCHIVE

Edited By Wallace A. Wyss

GT40 PHOTO ARCHIVE
FOREWORD BY BOB BONDURANT

Edited by Brian Winer and Wallace A. Wyss

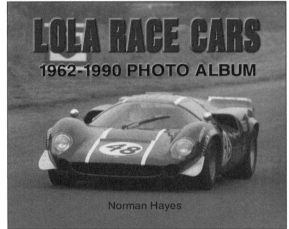

LOLA RACE CARS
1962-1990 PHOTO ALBUM

Norman Hayes

LE MANS 1950 PHOTO ARCHIVE
The Briggs Cunningham Campaign

Edited with introduction by Robert C. Auten • Photographs by Smith Hempstone Oliver

McLAREN
RACE CARS

1965 - 1996 PHOTO ALBUM
Norman Hayes

SEBRING 12-HOUR RACE 1970
PHOTO ARCHIVE

Edited by Robert C. Auten